351HR
OHIO 1966

GTO

Bill Holder & Phil Kunz

Motorbooks International
Publishers & Wholesalers ®

First published in 1997 by Motorbooks International Publishers & Wholesalers, 729 Prospect Avenue, PO Box 1, Osceola, WI 54020-0001

Motorbooks International books are also available at discounts in bulk quantity for industrial or sales-promotional use. For details write to Special Sales Manager at the Publisher's address

Library of Congress Cataloging-in-Publication Data Available
ISBN 0-7603-0360-6

On the front cover: The 1967 GTO was the last to feature stacked headlights. The functional single scoop Ram Air hood, which debuted in 1965, also appeared for the last time. This gorgeous 1967 GTO convertible is owned by Jim Amend.

On the frontispiece: For 1966, the GTO featured stacked headlights for the second straight year, and it had a significantly greater grille recess than on the 1965 model. Additional front-end styling came in the form of the broad horizontal slot in the bumper.

On the title page: The 1972 GTO design featured protruding creases, lower body chrome strips, and front fender air vents. This beautiful car, owned by Justin and Jeff Verburg, sports the optional hood-mounted tachometer and honeycomb wheels.

On the back cover: Produced between 1969 and 1971, Judges carried big horsepower and colorful graphics. This 1969 Judge belongs to Vic Bucci.

Printed in Hong Kong

CONTENTS

ACKNOWLEDGMENTS

We would like to thank the following for their technical assistance: Dan Greene, Asst. Media Relations Manager, Pontiac Motor Division; Richard L. Whaley; John Kocara; Andria and Pete Woodruff; Dick Kreiger; Ann Tasch; Greg Spencer; and Alan Lee.

The author would also like to thank the following owners who allowed the photographing of their magnificent GTOs and Judges for this book: Phil Woolpert ('64 GTO); Jim Shinsky and Allen Williams ('65 GTO); Bill Fetters, Ed Wimsatt, and Jim Hilliard ('66 GTO); Jim Amend ('67 GTO); Jim Barnett and Dave Johnson ('68 GTO); Paul George ('69 GTO); Cecil Lumley ('70 GTO); Frank Gramuglia ('71 GTO); Justin and Jeff Verburg ('72 GTO); Richard Whaley ('73/'74 GTOs); Vic Bucci ('69 Judge); Richard Whaley ('70 Judge); and Steve Salerno ('71 Judge).

The fourth GTO appeared in 1967, the last year of the so-called first generation. The 1967 GTO was the first Goat to carry a 400-ci powerplant. Previous GTOs were powered by the famous 389-ci engine.

INTRODUCTION

Having your muscle machine denoted with a three-letter identifier was a real popular technique during the 1960s. AMX, GTX, and, obviously, GTO come to mind.

The actual meaning of GTO is hard to figure but the letters did actually stand for something. Actually, the letter trio stands for "Grand Turismo Omologato." Sounds like it should be attached to some exotic foreign sports car, but the acronym in American terms covered a bevy of exotic Pontiac performance machines that many rate as the ultimate American muscle machines during the late 1960s and early 1970s.

The GTO nomenclature was popular for sure, but the model would acquire an interesting "Goat" name from many of its fans. Hard to figure the origin of that moniker, but it has stayed with the GTO through the years.

The GTO letters are extremely significant in the story of American muscle. Quite simply, the GTO was the first '60s muscle car to be merchandised as a high-performance machine for the masses. Granted, there were earlier performance cars, but they didn't fulfill this significant criteria.

The GTO moved in direct contradiction to the long-standing luxury image of the Pontiac Division. Granted, there had been monster high-horsepower powerplants, but there had never been a trim body to go with the significant ponies.

The first GTO was officially introduced in late 1963 as a special version of the Pontiac Tempest, and the GTO was immediately accepted by the public. In 1966, the GTO would find itself as a separate model.

The look and performance were exactly right for the time. The car's background is interesting in that this buildup of engine performance conflicted with Pontiac's backing away from its factory drag racing activities earlier in the year.

Also during this period there was a ban on standard powerplants of greater than 330 cubic inches (ci). There was obviously a problem if there was to be a big-engine GTO blaster. The solution was a bit on the sneaky side, to say the least. The solution was to make the big-engined GTO an option of the Tempest line.

In the years that followed, there were a series of big-block models that would demonstrate awesome 400-ci and 455-ci powerplants. But like other muscle car models of the period, it would all go away in the early 1970s.

The popularity of the GTO was exemplified by the so-called Judge model, which was introduced in 1969. Basically a highly detailed GTO, the schmaltzy three-year design has become a significant muscle collectable.

But for the exception of the Judge, flashy detailing was certainly not the style of the GTO. It was a great-looking machine to be sure, but the typical GTO was practically devoid of any flashy decals and stripes to differentiate the breed. Heck, even the awesome Tri-Power 389 powerplant was never denoted in any way.

Where competitors would splash flashy decals on the engine air cleaners denoting the engine's performance or cubic inches, such was never the case with the GTO.

With popularity sometimes come problems, and in the case of the GTO, it has been the building of fakes! Lots of fakes! Since the GTO was an option the first two years and the final three years, there was no way to differentiate the GTO by looking at the VIN (vehicle identification number) tag. They are easily forged, and you can believe that there are a lot more Tri-Powers in the 1990s than were ever built by Pontiac.

Is imitation the sincerest form of flattery? If you couldn't have a GTO, why not create one?

CHAPTER 1

THE FIRST GENERATION, 1964-1967

It's truly amazing how many famous models started out as options of a more established model, then became a separate model on their own, and finally sank back to being an option before they were discarded.

Such was the case with the first GTO, which started off as a part of the Tempest line. The oft-told story of how this first muscle car evolved deserves repeating as it was born in an era when Pontiac was backing out of racing and performance.

This was number one, the first-generation GTO, which appeared in 1964 with little fanfare. The model was actually an option of the LeMans line and available in both two-door coupe and convertible versions. Even though the first GTO, and the 1965 to follow, would both be LeMans options, the LeMans name would not appear anywhere on the car, only the GTO emblem. The two air intake castings were in place on the hood and gave an indication of the performance that was resting directly underneath. This first year, those intakes were strictly there for looks, but that would all change in the years to come, providing a Ram Air effect for increased performance. The GTO option could be ordered by checking the W62 option package.

GTO

9

More than anything else, the aspect that really got big-time attention was what was hiding under that stylish hood. It wasn't the first Pontiac multi-carb engine, but it certainly has become the most famous. It cost an extra $115.78 if checked on the option list, but it was well worth the extra coins. The initial vacuum setup for bringing the two outer carbs on-line for the '64 GTO didn't work that well. For that reason, many owners replaced the factory setup with a mechanical linkage arrangement. When perking to perfection, the Tri-Power engine was capable of 348 horses. There was also a four-barrel version of the powerplant producing a still-impressive 325 horses.

Boy, was the company ever surprised with what evolved with the model. The GTO set a new way of thinking about power and performance, a trend that would last until the early 1970s.

Here are the first four GTOs, normally referred to as the first generation. They've become muscle classics of the first order and will always hold their high place when the first muscle cars are recalled.

1964 GTO

It was lucky that the first GTO ever came to be in the first place. There was a Pontiac Motor Division (PMD) company restriction on any engine displacing more than 330 ci being carried as standard equipment. Somebody, though, forgot about offering such a performance engine as "optional" equipment. And when Oldsmobile offered such a performance powerplant as an optional offering

The interior of the '64 GTO had the look of a race car with classy bucket seats, an engine-turned aluminum instrument panel, custom steering wheel, and a console-mounted shifter. Optional gauges included a 7,000-rpm tach on the dash along with a manifold vacuum gauge, which was mounted on the sloped portion of the center console.

Does this look like a serious stoplight challenge? You'd better believe that more than one challenger looked over to see this and was then looking at the rear end of the GTO. The classy knock-off hub-style wheelcovers were a popular option with the first-year GTOs.

Was this exhaust treatment an attention-getter? You'd better believe it with that sweet rumble emerging from the tubes. There was a lot to hear since the 389-ci powerplant up front was pumping out plentiful ponies with a suspension system capable of putting them to the ground.

The rear profile of the first GTO was a squared-off design with the taillights stretching completely across the rear of the car. Back-up lights were buried in the outer corners of the bumper. Note the rear-deck GTO emblem. No problem with identification of this GTO.

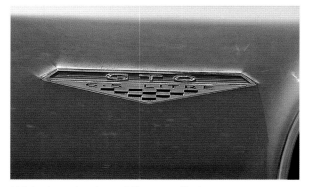

With that checkered-flag motif, there was no doubt about the racing and performance aspect of this machine. Tied with the GTO name, it didn't take long for the word to get around that this medallion meant something really special.

with the '64 Jetstar, Pontiac knew that it, too, had to respond.

The little loophole was pried open by Pontiac engineers who ended up wrangling a powerplant that exceeded the magic 330-ci figure by a significant 69 ci.

Due to the lateness of the decision, the GTO option was not a part of the initial LeMans sales literature. It has been rumored that some of the General Motors (GM) top brass didn't actually know about the option until it hit the showroom floor. And even though the initial GTO was only an option, the GTO name was the only name identification on the sheet metal, giving credence to the importance that was being given to the "first muscle car."

It was a battle of blooming GM performance for 1964 with the three letter/numeral machines battling each other. For Olds, it was the 442, and under the Pontiac banner, of course, was the GTO.

Without a doubt, the buyer got a machine that could pulverize the Saturday night opposition in any stoplight challenge. There were actually a pair of quick-revving 389-ci powerplants. They would remain in place, basically unchanged, for the first three years of the GTO. One version carried a high-capacity four-barrel carburetor, while the big-publicity version carried three two-barrel carbs, known as "Tri-Power."

Both versions of the famous engine carried special HO heads, high-performance valve springs, and a high-lift cam. The 325-horsepower (hp) four-barrel version was hooked up with a Rochester four-barrel (4GC) carb, while the heads were borrowed from the 421-ci Super Duty powerplants that came from Pontiac's earlier drag racing exploits. The torque was of a stump-pulling variety, being stated at the 428-foot-pounds figure. Interestingly, the same figure was quoted for the much-more publicized triple two-barrel version.

The standard drivetrain for this powerplant consisted of a column-mounted three-speed with a 3.23 axle ratio.

But what really caught the attention of the performance-minded was that so-called Tri-Power option. It was worth an additional 23 horsepower at 4,900 rpm, accomplished by an impressive row of three Rochester 2GC two-barrel carbs, which provided a total of 780 cubic feet per minute (cfm). For normal driving duties, the motor motivated along on only the center carb. Punch the pedal and the outer two came to life. Then stand back, and get the women and children off the streets!

Initially, that trio of carbs was operated with a vacuum setup, but it proved to be very impractical and would later be replaced with a mechanical linkage arrangement.

Pontiac actually had earlier tested the concept of putting a 389-ci engine with a 1963 Tempest. With that chassis in place, the concept didn't really work out, but when the updated '64 Tempest version came out, well, you know the results!

In a 1964 car test, *CAR LIFE* magazine tested a Tri-Power GTO and showed a super-impressive quarter-mile run of 14.8 seconds at 99 miles per hour. Zero-to-sixty was accomplished in only 6.6 seconds. Not bad considering that the curb weight of the machine was pushing 3,500 pounds.

Phil Woolpert of Bellbrook, Ohio, owns one of the best '64 GTOs in the land, and he drives the hauler a lot. "Man, there is nothing like the feel when those second two carbs come on-line when you punch the pedal. You are thrown solidly back in your seat, it's just great. But what I also really like is the sound of that howling engine as the RPMs come up."

Woolpert said that he used the highest-octane gas he could find, along with a lead additive. "I think this car burns cleaner than a new model with all the pollution gear," Woolpert explained.

With the Tri-Power, the standard tranny was a wide-ratio four-speed manual shifted with a floor-mounted unit. There was also a column-mounted two-speed and a montage of rear-end ratios, including 3.08, 3.36, 3.55, and 3.90. Reportedly, it was also possible to acquire 4.11 and 4.33 rear ends from the dealer.

Now, the most amazing aspect of the Tri-Power option: There was absolutely *no* identification on the engine or on the external sheet metal that three carbs were feeding those hungry cylinders. Even so, the real performance advocates saw the setup for what it was and bought it in great numbers.

Want more response under that right foot? It was available with a so-called "Roadability Group," which consisted of a beefier radiator, the Saf-T-Track limited-slip differential, and metallic brake linings.

This was just the start of the performance era, and the value of advertising horsepower and cubic inches on the sheet metal wasn't realized yet. In fact, the only such identification was quietly announced by a small front fender emblem that indicated that there were 6.5 liters under the hood, as if everybody knew that figure equated to 389 cubic inches.

GTO identifiers consisted of GTO emblems on the rear quarters, the left side of the grille, and the right side of the rear deck.

PMD also addressed the handling aspects of its new machine by upgrading the suspension system to include a four-link upper and lower rear control arm setup augmented with heavy-duty coil springs. The front end was stabilized with a 15/16-inch stabilizer bar.

Even though the GTO was establishing a name of its own, there wasn't a separate model carrying the name. Actually, you could acquire the GTO looks and power in the Tempest coupe, hardtop, or convertible version.

There were several aspects of the first GTO that would be found only on that model. One was the plastic-style steering wheel that appeared only that year, along with the GTO crest on the glovebox.

Even though they looked totally macho, those hood scoops were, unfortunately, not functional. The scoops carried closely spaced slots that gave the appearance of being workable. They culminated at the end of raised tunnels that reached toward the front of the hood. The twin separated scoops would reappear in the 1968 model, only this time they *would* be functional.

Yeah, the first GTO was basically a Tempest with the GTO trim work, but the sheet metal was perfect for the performance image it would project. Of course, there was the horizontal headlight front-end styling that would be changed the following year, but many GTO fans would liked to have seen it retained. Interestingly, the horizontal headlight styling would return to the GTO in the 1970s.

But what really set the GTO off from the many Tempests running down the road were the classy exhaust splitters, which emerged from under both rear corners of the machine. Put those together with the optional three-bar spinner custom wheel covers, and the nearly chromeless and totally stripeless side sheet metal, and the GTO acquired a unique pure-race look.

The interior was classy with bucket seats, a console which mounted a 7,000-rpm tach and a vacuum gauge, a Hurst shifter (with the manual transmission), and a race-style four-spoke wood steering wheel. It was definitely the topping on the cake for the first GTO. No wonder it sold like hotcakes!

There was a total of 32,450 GTOs built that inaugural year, with the hardtop being by far the most popular with 18,422 constructed. You would have thought differently, but the four-barrel-powerplant version outsold the Tri-Power almost three-to-one, actually 24,205 to 8,245.

1965 GTO

There's an old adage, "Don't change anything that's working good," but Pontiac didn't heed that advice and significant changes were instituted for GTO number two's body. The overall body lines were basically unchanged, but deviations abounded up front.

But when the shock of the redesign was over, most agreed that the changes were to their liking. The most noticeable change came from the now-vertical-stacked headlights. With the headlights removed from the twin grille scoops, the scoops now were more pronounced. There were also new front fenders which seemed to give the car more of an aggressive look. Minor changes to the rear end, with the chrome rolling around the body corners, gave the model more of a Grand Prix appearance.

The slot in the bumper was longer in the '65's front bumper. At the ends of the slot were the parking lights. Note the depth of the grille openings. The hood scoop was now singular, instead of the pair used for the '64 version. The scoop was centered with a vertical member separating the two sections. The new hood design had initially been planned for a 1966 introduction, but was moved up one year.

The overall look of the GTO was retained for the '65 GTO, but there were differences. First, the chrome strip through the grille openings was deleted, but the main change was the incorporation of the vertically stacked headlights. The same stylish crease the length of the body was still in place for the second GTO. It gave the body a rakish look interrupted only by the wheelwell bulges.

The twin hood scoops, which would reappear in later GTO versions, would be abandoned in favor of a single, centered unit.

There would be the first version of the Ram Air packages that would apply to the GTO in the years to come. A large gasket would encompass the three air cleaners of the Tri-Power setup, sealing it to the base of the hood. The setup allowed cold outside air to be directly funneled into the carbs. The Ram Air option, however, had to be bought over the dealership counter.

Probably the best judge of whether the changes were accepted would be a measure of sales. If that's the case, the changes went over like gangbusters as the sales vaulted to 75,352. The Tri-Power version also gained more fans with 20,547 of the buyers selecting that high-performance option. The hardtop was again, by far, the most popular GTO body style.

Maybe not surprisingly, the 1965 GTO was recently voted the most popular GTO of any of the 11 versions produced from 1964 to 1974!

Guess you could say that the second GTO really got into the spirit of the fledgling muscle-car era. Check out the optional Rally Cluster (RPO 504) option that provided the driver with a tach and schmaltzy gauge cluster.

The option sheet was long and interesting, offering air conditioning, a tilt steering wheel, power windows and seat, and an AM/FM radio. The steering wheel was now sporting three bars. And for a bit of a sporty look, there was a grab bar above the GTO emblem on the glovebox door.

Under the hood, the first look would mistakenly lead one to assume that no changes had

It didn't take long to figure out that cool outside air pumped directly into the carbs would increase the performance. Hence, this Ram Air tube could be acquired at the dealership to solidly close the connection to the hood scoop. It was never published by PMD as to exactly what the modification meant in terms of increased horsepower. Externally, the Tri-Power powerplant for 1965 looked identical to the previous year. The company announced, though, that it was worth an additional 12 horsepower from internal engine modifications. Put the pedal down to this engine and it was capable of 14-second quarters.

been made. Externally, that was close to the case, but with the innards, there were significant improvements that would provide additional ponies to the already potent package.

Looking first at the standard four-barrel carbed engine, the literature reported a 10-horse kick upward to 335 horses. The increased performance came from a higher-lift 288-degree cam, although the engine was still perking at the same 10.75:1 compression ratio.

There were also minor changes in the head and intake port deck heights. A Carter AFB four-barrel

was now the standard unit with this engine. The result was, in addition to the increased horsepower, a slight increase in torque to 431 foot-pounds.

The same three Rochester two-barrels were again in place for the Tri-Power version. Horsepower showed an increase of 12 to an impressive 360 figure. It also included the same changes just delineated for the standard version.

But if the performance gurus at PMD could have had their way, there would have been one more engine configuration, an awesome, dual-four-barrel carb version. Plans called for it to

A complete front-end revision for the 1966 GTO presented a new look for the third Goat. The grille recesses were deeper with the parking lights now mounted on the grille-opening mesh material. The grille recesses were also outlined with chrome trim. Long clean lines were the keynote of the 1966 GTO, with almost a straight line defining the overall look. It's little wonder that many rate the '66 model as the best GTO of them all. It's really hard to argue.

The rear-end treatment for the '65 GTO was completely revised. The rear taillight area stretched completely across the rear of the car and rolled around the corners of the rear fenders in a horizontally finned style. The locations for the rear-end GTO emblems were unchanged (on the lower-right rear deck and the rear quarters), and the Pontiac name was underlined in chrome.

A facelift for the dash of the '66 GTO was in place. The instruments were contained in a larger wood-colored area. All the gauges were directly in front of the driver. Mounted in the center console is the classy Hurst shifter for the available four-speed tranny. The standard three-speed transmission had the shifter mounted on the column. But if you were ordering a GTO, how could you not go with this setup? Identification of the 1966 GTO was carried in the interior with lettering on the left side of the glovebox. Note that there was also a sporty dash-mounted hand-hold for the front-seat passenger.

utilize a hotter cam and a cast-iron intake. For some unknown reason, it didn't come to pass. It certainly would have been a worthy adversary of similar units being fielded by Ford and Chrysler at the time. What might have been in this case would really have been something, and you just have to believe that it would have sold well.

In view of the tremendous popularity of GTO number two, there were two promotional versions flaunting the model, called the Hurst Hustler and the GeeTO Tiger.

The Hurst Hustler wasn't actually a factory option, but an identification that you belonged to the Hurst Hustler club, Hurst having a long-term

The rear-end design of the '66 model was completely new. First, a chrome strip outlined the rear of the deck lid. Then there was the new taillight treatment, which featured three raised channels. It was definitely a new look.

relationship with PMD. The membership involved the purchase of a set of special spinner Hurst wheels for one's GTO, and they looked positively smashing! The wheels were actually designed for the '65 GTO.

Along with the usual club membership card and jacket patch came three Hurst Hustler emblems that could be placed on the car. The normal location was on the rear deck directly across from the GTO emblem. And even though the wheels could roughly be called aftermarket items,

they are still respected as pretty much "factory" by car show judges.

The so-called GeeTO Tiger was a dashing GTO giveaway model that was gold in color, carrying a wide orange stripe on the lower body between the wheelwells. Then there was the gold plating that covered the Hurst wheels and shifter. It was definitely a one-of-a-kind with the original model still existing.

For the national advertising campaign, a popular showroom technique for the '65 GTO was to

A low look at the '66 GTO reveals one of the reasons for its outstanding handling. The rear sway bar in the differential area of the rear end is clearly visible from this angle.

hang an orange-and-black tiger tail from the fuel filler door protruding out on the right side of the license plate. The cute technique resulted in huge exposure in national magazines and on television.

1966 GTO

For the GTO's third year, the competition was hot and heavy for the up-and-running GTO. First, there was another triple-carb model in the Olds 442, along with the SS396 Chevelle and the Buick Gran Sport.

The final year for the awesome Tri-Power powerplant was 1966. The final 389 could also be equipped with the XS performance option and included such items as stiffer valve springs and a high-lift cam. The package required dealer installation.

But never fear, the GTO was up to the challenge. It was first addressed with the significant restyling. This started with the grille design, which now had its two sections deeply recessed. The parking lights were moved from the lower bumper location to the outside of the grilles, and the GTO emblem filled the remaining space in the left grille. The Pontiac crest was centered on the front of the hood, just forward of the single scoop location.

Other trim changes included decreasing the size of the GTO emblem on the right side of the trunk. Although there was again no chrome detailing on the sides of the GTO (which was now in its first year as a full-fledged model), the design was accentuated by a low body crease that folded down to the wide chrome lower body stripe.

The same engines were carried over for year three, but this would be the 389-ci powerplant's last curtain call. It was getting to the point that you had to start the engine displacement figure with a "four" in this performance big-block era.

The Tri-Power engine was being quoted with the same horsepower figure, although the center carburetor had been slightly enlarged. It was this center carb that the engine used until the throttle was punched. Then the two outside slaved carbs were brought into action. It was pretty high-tech stuff for the time.

Again, PMD quietly offered an engine upgrade option, the so-called XS option, which

The front end of the '67 GTO changed little from the previous year with the same twin-grille configuration. The parking lights were still located in the grille openings, but the texture of the grille was of a wider pattern. From the side, it was difficult to discern much difference between the '66 and the '67 GTO. The side sheet metal, though, was cleaned up with the Pontiac emblem lowered to the lower chrome strip. The functional Ram Air hood was still in place for 1967. As with earlier versions, the configuration allowed a solid connection to be made between the hood and carburetor. This was the final year for this scoop configuration, as the following years had a pair of separated scoops.

contained the functional Ram Air system that had been offered the year earlier, but this year it went one step further. There was now a new cam and new valve springs. In order to qualify for the XS option, is was necessary to check off the M21 four-speed, 4.33 rear-end gearing, and several other mandatory options.

An interesting option made its bow with the '66 Goat in the form of molded red plastic front-inner-fender liners. The liners would also appear in performance versions of the Olds 442s of the same period. The liners, though, would only be available on the GTO through the 1967 model year.

1967 GTO

It seemed that everything was going well with the new image that had been created for the GTO. The Tiger theme had become the standard by which the model had become known and everything appeared rosy. Rosy, that is, except on the top floors of General Motors corporate offices. Tiger stripes were no longer in vogue, and a new theme for GTO number four was ordered.

For those who loved the performance implications of the model, the order that came down from on high was that all multi-carb powerplants were to be discontinued. In fact, it was made very clear that the GTO was *not* to be advertised with racing nor promoting an "aggressive driving"

The stacked headlight arrangement that first appeared on the 1965 GTO continued on the 1967 Goat. The lights were completely embedded in a chrome housing that blended into the straight body lines.

theme. Things had changed in a big way, but the GTO would adapt.

The new standard engine for the Goat would move up 11 cubic inches to the magic 400 figure, but it just didn't seem to have the charisma of the 389 number, a displacement that had been Pontiac's alone. The 400 number would also find its way into a number of other General Motors models.

Actually, though, it was still the same old 389, which had been slightly punched out to achieve the new displacement. A number of other improvements were made to the new engine, including more efficient cylinder heads. They incorporated larger intake and exhaust valves with a new intake manifold designed to accept the sin-

gle Rochester Quadrajet carburetor, which would become the standard for the new mill.

A number of different versions of the engine were available, depending on customer preferences. Interestingly, a low-power version of the engine was offered, the first time such an engine was offered with the GTO. The 255-horsepower two-barrel carb version featured lower compression and smaller valves, with fuel economy being the highlight of the design. Guess you could say that you got the best of two worlds with the GTO performance image on the outside, but fewer trips to the gas pump for the billfold.

But for most, it would have been sacrilegious not to have the appropriate ponies in place for

Many GTOs of the era carried this dramatic Hurst spoked-style wheel. It was available in both gold and silver. The Hurst company emblem was carried on the center hub.

that famous sheet metal. It's interesting that the standard 400 engine bore a large similarity to the 1966 single four-barrel 389 and was rated at 335 horsepower. The similarity was understandable since it used many of the same internal components from the '66 version.

A potent, new, 360-horse, 400 HO version was next up the 1967 GTO performance family tree, and it was a killer. Drawing on some older classic Pontiac technology, the headers were quite similar to the earlier Super Duty versions of the early 1960s. A hotter cam and open-element air cleaner also added to the characteristics of the engine that would soon have performance enthusiasts proclaiming its virtues.

The factory literature really featured this powerplant with these words: "You can order the 360-HP Quadra-Power 400. New heads, new combustion chamber design, bigger valves, enlarged ports, and more efficient runners." The words had to appeal big-time to the performance-minded, of which there were many during this exciting muscle-car period.

The Ram Air nomenclature would make its presence known for the first time with the top engine for '67. Even though it wasn't breathing through three two-barrel carbs, the had-to-be-more-than-360-

horse engine used the tub-enclosed four-barrel to significant advantage. Other goodies included special valves and valve springs and the potent 744 cam. To acquire these big horses, it cost the customer a minimal $263.30 extra.

With a number of race-specific options that were available, it was possible to actually assemble a turn-key drag car right on the dealership floor. Such items as a heavy-duty frame, heavy-duty shocks and springs and radiator, special clutch fan, heavy-duty Saf-T-Track rear end, and others were available. The result was a machine capable of running in the mid-12s.

It's interesting to review how the four different 400 powerplants were viewed by the public. It was no contest, with the vast majority of the 81,722 buyers (64,177 to be exact) checking off the standard 400. For the two-barrel 400, 2,967 people bought it. With the performance versions, the 400 HO was the leading choice with 13,827 making that selection, while only 751 bought the expensive Ram Air version.

Guess it's understandable why that potent version is such a rare collectable in the 1990s. By the way, the fact that you were carrying a Ram Air engine under the hood was not announced on the sheet metal, an amazing situation with the growing interest in performance. That external recognition would come later in the decade.

Safety and handling got significant attention with the revised Goat, as it got new 14-inch front power disc brakes and an energy-absorbing steering wheel. It would also acquire, in option form, shoulder seat belts and a so-called Safeguard Speedometer, which let out a warning buzz when the speed exceeded a preset speed.

Changes on the '67 Goat weren't just under the hood. The outside appearance also presented a completely different look, most of it coming with the completely revised rear end. Recall that the '66 GTO had taillights in the form of three elongated slots on each side of the vertical rear panel.

With this year's version, there were now eight rear lights, four on each side, which were artfully flared into the rear flat area.

The triple carbs were gone after GTO's first three years, but the power was still plentiful with the 400 HO powerplant shown here. The potent mill was rated at 360 horses and carried a special valvetrain and cam. Performance didn't miss a beat with the changing of the powertrain guard.

Also, the GTO medallion, which had previously rested on the front quarters, was now lowered onto the rocker panel chrome trim piece, which was wider than the year before. There was no particular reason for the move, but it did give the side sheet metal a clean look, with the exception of the GTO lettering, which was retained on the rear quarter. The grille treatment was basically unchanged from the '66 version, as was the interior.

One new item for '67 was the smashing, hood-mounted tach. It came down to the point that to have a real GTO, you had to have the 8,000-rpm dial, which sat directly in front of the driver. And of course, it was illuminated at night.

After initially being a dealer-installed option, its popularity would quickly cause it to become a factory option.

"Our hood-mounted tach option. You don't know what shifting is, unless you have one. Dealer installed," was the way the sales brochures described this nifty option.

The muscle-car era was coming on strong, and the '67 GTO was right in the middle of it. In this period advertisement, the main discussion was on the powerplants and their performance. Note that the advertisement also mentioned the hood-mounted tach availability.

The Great One. GTO Hardtop. Need we say more?

Pontiac Motor Division

The incomparable GTO for '67 comes with 400 cubic inches of engine under a magnificently refined new skin. Or you can order the 255-hp version or the new 360-hp Quadra-Power Four Hundred. And for the first time you can order your GTO with our three-speed Turbo Hydra-Matic.

Our revolutionary 165-hp Overhead Cam Six is standard on all Le Mans and Tempests. You can specify the 215-hp 4-bbl version, a spirited 250-hp regular gas V-8 or its 285-hp premium gas cousin. Or you can step into the neatest grand touring car this side of the Atlantic with our OHC 6 Sprint package. Also new for this year—Executive and Tempest Safari wagons with walnut wood grain styled sides. All this plus the road-hugging security of Wide-Track on every Pontiac we make. See your Pontiac dealer right now.

Wide-Track Pontiac/67

You can add full fidelity sound by ordering our eight-track stereo tape player.

Leave it to Pontiac to come up with it first: now you can order a hood-mounted tach!

New for 1967, the hood-located instrument was a big hit. It started out as a dealer-installed option, but its popularity made it a factory option after only a couple months. The tach measured revs up to 8,000 rpm.

Some changes were made on the rear end of the '67 GTO. The biggest change came with the taillight design, which had a new stacked layout with four on each side.

If you see a '67 GTO carrying what appears to be aftermarket Hurst spoked wheels, that appearance isn't quite what it appears.

With the relationship between Pontiac and Hurst still very strong, it was possible to actually have dealers install the flashy Hurst wheels, which could be acquired in either chrome or gold. Many owners also mounted Hurst emblems on their GTOs.

Through its early years, the GTO had always been noted for its stylish and revolutionary wheels. With the '67 GTO, the new Rally II wheel continued the trend. The five-spoke design also featured five cooling slots and the tightly centered, deeply recessed, color-coated lug nuts. Combined with the F70x14 redline tires, the continuation of the GTO was even more enhanced.

CHAPTER 2

THE SECOND GENERATION, 1968-1972

Y ou'd have to say that the 1968 GTO was a new breed of cat, which made it a worthy model to introduce the GTO's second generation. In terms of styling, innovations, and performance, it was definitely a tough act to follow.

Most consider that the unofficial second generation lasted through the 1972 model, when the performance era would effectively end, taking the GTO down with it. Even though there would be two more models (1973 and 1974) carrying the GTO emblem, the GTO that America had learned to know and love was gone.

Here are the GTOs of generation two, a number of which sported the most powerful engines yet.

The '68 Goat received the *Motor Trend* Car of the Year award, and looking at its sleek design, it's not hard to understand the honor. Another magazine indicated that "The GTO is still the hands-down leader of the super cars." A huge design innovation hit the '68 GTO with the introduction of the Endura bumper. The molded appearance of the front end looked like it had been accomplished by a rod shop. It was really hard to determine where the sheet metal ended and the front bumper started.

GTO

The Ram Air I 400 for 1968 was the king of the hill for a time. It produced an impressive 360 horsepower. Later in the model year, the Ram Air II would be introduced, an awesome powerplant which could provide an additional 10 ponies.

1968 GTO

The material was called Endura and it served as the basis for the new bumper design for the 1968 Goat. With its application to the new front-end design, the flexible, space-age material was able to absorb low-speed front-end impacts and bounce back to its original shape. Also, the characteristics of the material actually allowed the car to bounce away from the object it encountered. It was certainly a dramatic improvement over the previous metal front ends.

But the stylists also loved the material since it allowed the coloring of the bumper to match the shade of the body itself, along with providing a smoother overall appearance. In fact, it was hard to tell where the front bumper ended and the sheet metal of the front fenders began.

The body was shortened by 3 inches from its 1967 length, with more bulging around the wheelwell openings. GTO number five was really starting to have a race car look about it. That racy look was continued by the use of a GTO decal (instead of a chrome emblem) on the rear quarters. Another nice touch was the use of a Pontiac-shaped marker light immediately aft of the GTO decal. There were still chrome emblems, though, on the rear deck and inside the left front grille opening.

To go along with the clean front-end look were the optional concealed headlights, whose doors were vacuum-operated. After three years with vertically stacked headlights, the designers went back to the original 1964 design with the horizontal configuration.

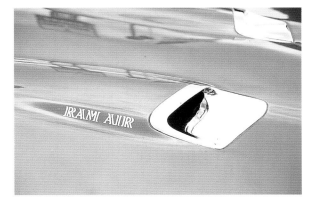

The twin, separated hood scoops were functional with the '68 Ram Air I powerplant and carried "Ram Air" nomenclature on the outside of each scoop.

There was considerable redesign done on the dash with the wood paneling now extending completely across its breadth. Also, the number of dials was reduced to three from the previous four. Also note the Dual-Gate Hurst shifter for the new Turbo Hydra-Matic tranny.

For the GTO design for 1969, the name of the game was again the new Endura bumper, which would assume its original shape after an impact.

The '68 Goat was again voted the Car of the Year, a fact that PMD flaunted in the company literature. "But with a car like this, what did you expect?" the company said.

Considerable changes were also made in the treatment of both the ends of the machine. The taillights were moved into the bumper, while up front, the parking lights assumed their new position outside the grille.

In another bold option that was available, the headlights were hidden in the blackout-grille openings with the lids opening when the lights were activated. The centered single hood scoop of the previous year had been dropped for the twin scoops, which would continue for a number of the following years.

The changes sat well with the buying public and the car magazines of the period, with *Motor Trend* magazine voting the model the 1968 Car of the Year.

Horsepower was plentiful from three monster powerplants. First, the standard 400-ci powerplant produced 350 horsepower at 5,000 rpm with an awesome 444 foot-pounds of torque. A series of automatic and manual transmissions, along with numerous rear-end ratios, could be assembled for just about every performance fantasy.

You had to plunk down an additional $237 for the Turbo Hydra-Matic, or $184 for a manual tranny. The Saf-T-Track rear end was a minimal $63.

The standard 400 was followed by the 400 HO, which featured a different cam, Ram Air style exhaust manifold, different carburetor jettings, and a 10.75:1 compression ratio. It was followed by the Ram Air 400 engine, which carried the same HO goodies in addition to the Ram Air pans.

Then, in March of 1968, Pontiac kicked up the number again, replacing the Ram Air 400 engine with a new Ram Air II powerplant, which sported a hotter cam, new round-port heads, round exhaust ports, a Rochester Quadrajet carburetor, hydraulic cam, and forged aluminum pistons. The engine sported a 4.12-inch bore and 3.75-inch stroke. With its 366 willing ponies, it was ready for the drag strip right off the showroom floor. Engine performance was measured with a sporty, hood-mounted 8,000-rpm tach, the same installation that was used on the Firebird.

The '68 Ram Air II was an awesome performer and has been rated by GTO experts as one of the best ever built. The quick-revving mill made this machine a low-14-second performer on street tires at almost 100 miles per hour. It was also capable of 7.4-second performance in a 0-60-miles-per-hour dash.

An interesting touch with the Ram Air engines was the fact that the induction systems, which connected the hood scoops to the top of the carburetor, were not installed at the factory but arrived in the trunk for dealer installation. The scoops were also painted by the dealer to match the car's color.

But if you didn't want performance quite up to the dynamite looks of the sheet metal, there was a low-power 400-ci mill hooked up with a two-barrel carburetor. Performance, though, was a surprising 265 horses with only

The rear-end treatment was also entirely revised for the fifth GTO, with the taillights now firmly embedded in the outside of the bumper. It continued the clean, uncluttered look of the front end. Rear-end identification for the '68 GTO consisted of the rear-quarter GTO decal accompanied by the triangular Pontiac emblem. The chrome GTO emblem was continued on the right corner of the rear deck.

With its bright red lettering, there was no mistaking that this '69 Pontiac was indeed a GTO. The lettering had a black background in the shape of the Pontiac emblem and was outlined in chrome.

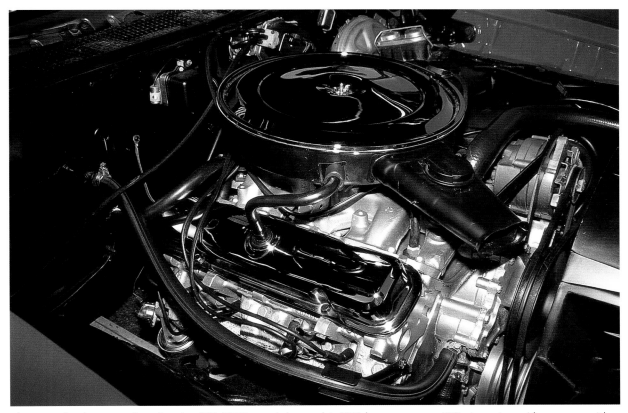

The standard powerplant for the '69 GTO model was this 350-horsepower, 400-ci version. Also, even with the performance-image GTO name, it was possible to acquire a two-barrel-carbed 400 with a 265-horsepower rating.

an 8.6:1 compression ratio. You have to wonder, though, why anyone would buy maybe the best-looking muscle car ever built with a LO-PO powerplant. Some 2,841 customers did make the purchase, however.

The popular dual-gate shifter would see its final year with the 1968 GTO, also having been available with the 1967 model.

PMD really had its act together with this fifth GTO as it was the bestseller of all the Goats. The striking total was 87,684, with the hardtop being the bestseller as expected at 77,704 units. Even though the GTO was supposedly a performance machine of the first order, few buyers chose the performance engine. Maybe they figured that the standard 400-ci engine was powerful enough with a vast majority of 73,793 making the low-power choice.

1969 GTO

For the final GTO of the decade, there were appreciable changes made in the looks department, with a majority of them occurring in the rear end.

First of all, the taillights were no longer centered in the bumpers but carried lenses with brightmetal trim moldings and reached around the rear quarters. The front-end appearance remained basically unchanged with the popular Endura rubber nose; the long, sweeping hood carrying the optional tach and Ram Air scoop openings; hidden headlights; and long, sweeping front

A comparison with the rear ends of the '69 GTO (left) and the '68 model shows the sizable differences between the pair. It's easy to note the redesign for '69 as the '68 model had the taillights completely enclosed by the bumper.

fenders. A bright chrome strip traverses the center of both grille openings.

Body style offerings included both the convertible and hardtop, with the hardtop being the huge favorite, 77,704 to a paltry 9,980 for the rag top. (The year also marked the introduction of a new GTO, the Judge, which will be addressed separately in Chapter 5.)

Four powerplants were available this year: the standard 400 four-barrel, a 400 two-barrel, the Ram Air III, and Ram Air IV engines. The overall favorite was a resounding go for the standard 400, probably a reflection of the added cost for the Ram Air versions with only a small increase in horsepower.

The standard powerplant was a 350-horsepower version equipped with a four-barrel, with the low-power two-barrel version generating 265 horses. Nineteen sixty-nine would be the final year for that low-power engine.

The front grille for the '69 Goat was slightly changed from the previous year with the addition of a centered chrome strip. The GTO emblem was moved more toward the center of the car and was lowered in position.

The Ram Air III engine utilized a D-Port head style and a Rochester Quadrajet carburetor. It made 366 horsepower and was denoted with Ram Air decals on the functional hood scoops. The Ram Air III was another rocket slightly faster than the Ram Air II of the previous year, showing a best quarter-mile clocking of 14.10 seconds. It also made the same 445 foot-pounds of torque as the '68 Ram Air II, but made this significant twisting power at 200 fewer rpm, at 3,600 rpm.

But ask any Goat performance enthusiast and you'll quickly learn that the Ram Air IV was the ultimate of the 400 engines, bar none! For street performance, it was beautifully balanced and a terror at any confrontation. The fact that it was rated at only 4 horsepower over the Ram Air III powerplant was a joke, with everybody knowing its actual rating was well over 400 horses.

Reportedly, the '69 Ram Air IV was the fastest of all the muscle GTO versions. This model was capable of 6.6-second performance from 0 to 60 miles per hour, but the real eye-raiser was its quarter-mile clocking of 13.90 seconds at a super-impressive 101.5 miles per hour. The runs were made using a close-ratio M21 transmission and a 3.90 rear end. The Ram Air III wasn't much off that pace, running the quarter in 14.10 seconds at 98.20 miles per hour.

During this period, it was those kinds of numbers that were selling performance cars. The com-

The rear-end treatment for the '69 Goat was redesigned for the last model year of the decade. The taillights were dropped into openings in the bumper. There were two horizontally stacked lights on each side.

petition was tough, even within General Motors, with the awesome Olds 442 W machines, the Gran Sport Buicks, and big-block 396-ci Chevys.

Just listening to the powerful sounds at the tailpipe told of the engine's wilder cam. With its forged pistons, polished valves, a high-rise aluminum intake, and advanced round-port heads, it could really get the job done. The magnificent mill's presence was announced by a Ram Air IV decal on the outside of each hood scoop. And you better believe that it really increases the value of these cars with collectors in the 1990s.

Rumors abounded during this time period about a killer Ram Air V powerplant, and there was really a factory effort toward the development of such an engine, a powerplant that would take Pontiac performance to the next level.

Though racing was still a bad word in the PMD corporate towers, a quiet effort was carried out during the late 1960s under the guidance of John DeLorean. The Ram Air V actually had Ford roots in the form of a 427-ci engine that was being used in national stock car racing.

Using that technology as a starting point, the project began in 1966 and evolved into two different configurations. First, there was 428-ci version with a pair of four-barrel carbs, while a 400-ci version sported a single four-barrel. Reportedly, the 428-ci version was capable of a heart-rendering 510 horsepower using a Ram Air IV camshaft and solid lifters. Release of that engine for the GTO would possibly have made the Goat the ultimate muscle car.

The engineers knew, though, there was no way the engine would ever be approved for production vehicles, and it wouldn't be long before the entire effort would be canceled. Surprisingly, though, there were some 500 Ram Air V engines built, 100 of the 428-ci versions and the remainder

The Ram Air engines for 1969 incorporated this unique foam closure unit atop the air cleaner. The Ram Air III and IV were rated at 366 and 370 horsepower, respectively. Those in the know would tell you that those ratings were extremely underrated. On the hood, Ram Air IV lettering on the functional scoops of the '69 Goat told of one of Pontiac's most potent mills ever. The engine featured forged pistons, a wild cam, aluminum intake manifold, and round-port heads.

being the 400-ci types. Most of the engines went to oval-track racers, but a few of them are still reportedly floating around.

But let's get back to the production '69 GTO, a model that greatly resembled the Goat of a year earlier. It would take a real Goat expert to differentiate between the pair. The sheet metal on the '69 Goat was essentially the same as the previous year except for the addition of some new trim and detailing. The optional concealed headlights were still peering at you as a part of the still-in-place Endura bumper.

There was, however, a slight change in the grille texture pattern, but the biggest visual differ-

ence came with the addition of a horizontal chrome strip through the middle of the grille.

The parking lights were completely redesigned and located directly beneath the headlight doors. They were nicely set off with crisscrossing chrome stripes. With a step up to modern times, the vent windows were finally eliminated in

The GTO wasn't the only Pontiac performance machine for 1969. This period advertisement shows the GTO in the center. Up front is the potent Firebird (note the GTO-like twin hood scoops), and the Grand Prix is in the rear.

We'd like to put in a good word for hoods.

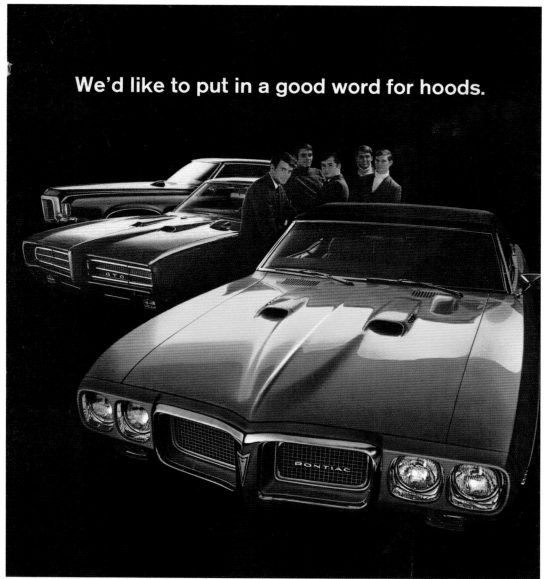

Why not? We've got the toughest looking in the business.

Take that sweep of metal on the '69 Pontiac Grand Prix. You won't find a longer stretch from Sing Sing to Alcatraz.

The two bulges on Firebird 400 and GTO are pretty unsubtle, too. They're air scoops. Functional when you order Ram Air.

Now, you can order a tach for each of these hoods. And they'll look tougher. But let's face it. No hood's complete without a persuader.

Pontiac has them.

Grand Prix's is a standard 350-horse, 400-cubic-inch V-8. Or specify a 370- or 390-horse 428-cube V-8.

Firebird 400 has a 330-horse, 400-cubic-inch V-8 standard. You get even more im-pressive statistics when you order the H.O. or Ram Air IV version.

GTO started it all. Remember? A 350-horse, 400-cubic-inch V-8 is standard. A 366-hp V-8 and a 370-hp Ram Air IV await your order.

Obviously, this is no year to go around bad-mouthing Pontiac's hoods.

GM
MARK OF EXCELLENCE
Pontiac Motor Division

The rear-end design for the '70 GTO went back to an earlier look, with the taillights again being installed in the rear bumper. A decal identified the GTO on the rear deck, but interestingly, the rear-quarter identification had been deleted.

this Goat, never to reappear. The classy hood-mounted tach was again in place.

The popularity of the last-of-the-decade GTO continued its downward spiral, but sales were still somewhat strong at 72,287. The hardtop accounted for 64,851 of the total, but most turned away from the performance powerplants, with only 700 buying the Ram Air IV mill. It's easy to understand why these rare versions are so highly sought after by collectors in the 1990s.

1970 GTO

Although performance and style were the key words for the first GTO of the new decade—the

The displacement of the onboard powerplant was carried on some '70 GTOs beneath the GTO decal. In this case, the top-gun 455 powerplant was in place.

The macho look of the earlier GTO powerplants was fading along with their performance. Note the use of the painted valve covers instead of the long-standing chrome pieces. The standard engine for the '71 Goat was this 400-ci mill, which had seen its compression ratio lowered to only 8.2:1 from its previous 10.25:1 figure.

company called it "The Humbler"—safety was also rising in importance. Side protection was the area of emphasis with the installation of a beefy new side-guard door beam.

Then, too, there was the departure of two individuals who had meant so much to the birth and nurturing of the GTO through its formative years. First, John DeLorean left Pontiac to become the head man at Chevrolet, while GTO advertising guru Jim Wangers also departed. But never mind, the effect on the 1970 GTO apparently wouldn't be felt as this model is still rated as one of the best of the Goat herd.

There were those who argued, though, that the design was starting to move away from its lean-and-mean look to more of a luxury look. The hideaway headlights were dropped (possibly mostly because of mechanical problems) with a return to the exposed-light look. The lights were more recessed with a Frenched-in look.

The big news, though, for this GTO was the introduction of a 455-ci powerplant for the first time. The big-block would be around through the 1973 GTO, only in greatly reduced-power versions. The 455 (which was quoted with both 360- and 370-horse horsepower ratings) was available

This early factory photo of the '70 GTO illustrates the complete redo of the front end. The chrome had been illuminated, and the Endura bumper was used to perfection for the uncluttered clean look. The twin-grille design was still there, but it sure had taken on a completely different look.

with both three- and four-speed manual and the Turbo Hydra-Matic transmissions. Interestingly, the horsepower rating of this big-block mill was about the same as the Ram Air IV engine, which was also an option.

It was also possible to order the Ram Air equipment with the 455 big-block, but there were no internal engine changes made when that choice was made. The heritage of that 455 is interesting in that its roots were from the 428-ci engine, which was used in the larger GM cars. It didn't take much of an overbore and stroking to come up with the additional 27-ci increase. The engine also incorporated four-bolt mains, larger valves, and the 1969 Ram Air 400 camshaft.

For some reason, the new big-block wasn't making the horsepower expected from its greater displacement. Rated at "only" 360 horsepower, the figure was surprisingly lower than both of the Ram Air 400-ci powerplants. Its advantage came with its significant torque capability, but it didn't have the punch in the quarter-mile runs with 96-mile-per-hour performance, which took about 15 seconds to achieve.

The awesome Ram Air IV engine, which cost the buyer a hefty $558 extra, was almost identical to the Ram Air IV of 1969, with the exception of the compression ratio being dropped from 10.75 to 10.50:1. Was this the first clue to the massive downgrade that was just over the horizon? The Ram Air III (366 horsepower) and the standard 400 engine (rated at 350 horsepower) gave the buyer just about any performance engine desired.

The factory sales booklets, though, told of what was to come as the suspension system was mentioned more prominently than the awesome powerplants that were available. It would also be

The classy side-body sculpting of the '71 GTO is really evident from this side view. The protruding creases are most noticeable over the front and rear wheelwells. The look was really accentuated with the chrome strip along the lower body and the front-quarter GTO decal. The optional honeycomb wheel was available for the '71 model year and gave the GTO a bit of a different look. Was it moving away from the race-appearance Rally wheels? Could be, as handling and roadability were becoming the key advertising claims and this wheel just seemed to fit in.

the first year for the rear sway bar.

The 1970 GTO bore an amazing similarity to PMD's pony car, the Firebird. In fact, more than one buyer made the wrong identification because of the look-alike grille designs. With the exception of the single headlights on the Firebird, the two front-end treatments were almost identical.

Compared to the long, narrow grille openings of the '69 GTO, the 1970 version was much more egg-shaped. The overall look seemed to integrate nicely with the twin hood scoops, which were basically unchanged from the previous model year.

The chrome GTO body identifications were in their normal right rear deck and left grille locations, but the side emblems were again carried in decal formats.

The body styling of the 1970 GTO was a bit more rounded and conservative than the squared-off look of the previous designs. It seemed to be a sign of the times, but for some reason, the buying public wasn't buying it at all!

Including the Judge versions, there were only 40,149 GTOs produced during this model year, down dramatically from the 1969 total. The hard-top version accounted for about 90 percent of the sales at 36,366 sold. The performance downturn was also vividly illustrated as 18,148 selected the standard 400-ci powerplant. The Ram Air IV saw only 767 buyers, while the new 455-ci engine got 3,747 purchasers. The change was on the way, and the GTO would feel the new environment in the very near future.

It was hard to recognize the GTO in 1971 from the previous year. The look was sure different, mostly from the new twin-scoop treatment. The location had moved forward, and the shape was now more of a long slot. Many said it looked more like a Firebird.

1971 GTO

There were conflicting messages governing the production of performance cars for the 1971 model year. Performance was on a downturn, but not yet dead, but whatever punch was provided also had to meet the strenuous new emission requirements that were quickly gaining national favor.

Moving completely against that conservative thinking was a rumor about a new performance powerplant that might appear in the '71 GTO. Reportedly, Pontiac was developing a new, aluminum 427-ci engine that would be rated at an unbelievable 640 horsepower. Of course, it never would come to pass, but it made interesting copy during the period for the car magazines, who were striving to keep up the interest in street perfor-

Even though performance was being dropped out of the GTO's publicity and advertising, the company still saw fit to flaunt the fact that a big-block could be acquired in the '71 Goat. The displacement figure was carried under the front-quarter GTO decal, as shown here.

Compared to the redone front end, less-changed on the '71 Goat was the rear end, which was very similar to the previous year's model. The taillights were again embedded in the rear bumper with the rear-deck decal identification. Note the deck-mounted rear-deck spoiler.

mance. An interesting note is that two years later, Pontiac would field the awesome 455 Super Duty powerplant in the 1973-74 Firebird and Trans Am.

Instead of any increases under Pontiac hoods, the actual situation was that the power went the other way. The decrease was actually dictated from an outside source, the federal government requirement that all engines would have to be able to function on unleaded or low-lead gasoline.

General Motors decided that the best place to bring its engines into compatibility with the new low-power petrol was to lower the compression ratios. Needless to say, it required a significant lowering of compression. For the 455-ci engines, the drop descended to a lowly 8.4:1,

while it took an additional .2 to accomplish the same effect on the 400-ci engines.

Now figure this phenomenon: In a period when the performance was obviously on the downturn, PMD suddenly started flaunting the 455 HO designation on the top of the engine's air cleaner. That trend would continue through the 1972 model.

Other changes to the 455 HO (which added $137 to the sticker) were also required, including the sealing of the carburetor mixture ratio, and a new sensor arrangement which shut the automatic choke off more quickly during start-up. With these changes in the name of economy, performance enthusiasts dreaded to hear what effect it would

The bumper-enclosed taillights were the thing again for the '72 GTO. The twin exhaust stacks emerged this year from the right side just behind the right rear wheel, just the way they did with the first GTO.

have on quarter-mile clockings. For sure, the good old days with high-13-second runs would definitely be a thing of the past.

Even though the powerplants' oomph was definitely on the wane, there was an interesting statement made by the company in the showroom handouts: "Despite the fact that the 455 engines now runs on low-lead gas, the new '71 GTOs actually outperform their predecessors." That's exactly what they said!

The Ram Air nomenclature that had identified the previous big-power engines was gone, even though the Ram Air lettering was still continued on the hood scoops. The differences, though, were that these Ram Air systems could not be driver-controlled. But when the hood was closed, the hood air duct was sealed to the air cleaner snorkels. The setup would also be offered through 1972 models.

What it actually meant in terms of horsepower was a drop to 300 for the 400 engines (down from 350 of a year earlier), and the 455 HO only showed 335 horsepower (a considerable drop from the 370 horsepower of 1970). But what made things look even worse came from the fact that the government started requiring the companies to also quote the horsepower in net values, which were quoted lower than the gross numbers.

PMD, though, did its best to compensate for the decreased compression by creating better acceleration by lowering the gear ratios and incorporating the high-rise aluminum Ram Air IV intake. Work was also done on the carb to improve the throttle response. Also, the Rally Sport shifter enabled improved shifting capability. So it wasn't quite as bad as it seemed from the performance point-of-view, and surprisingly, some tests showed that 455 HO machines were still capable of 14-second quarter-mile performance. Experts noted that the capability came from the wide torque band demonstrated by the still-potent powerplant.

There was a wide variety of engine/transmission GTO possibilities, with three- and four-speed manual and Turbo Hydra-Matics available with both the 400 and 455 HO, and with just the automatic coming with the standard 455 engine.

Styling-wise, the '71 Goat took on a completely new look on the front end. It looked entirely different from the previous year, actually more racy than the '70 model, even though it sure couldn't back it up under the hood, which by the way, could be locked down with race-style hood tie-downs.

The first aspect of the new front end was the relocating of the long-standing twin hood scoops. With this model, they were pulled far forward on the hood and increased considerably in size. Where the '70 versions were more oval in shape, the '71 scoops were long, horizontal slots and almost stretched across the breadth of the front part of the hood. Only a small band of sheet metal separated them. They looked totally awesome!

Then there was that long snout nose that gave the model a completely new look. The new grille didn't flow into the rest of the body styling like the '70 Goat, instead looking more like it had been stuck on as an afterthought. It had its critics, but it also had an ample number of admirers.

The grille design aligned with the hood scoops, with the large grille openings still somewhat maintaining the GTO heritage. The openings were blacked out and carried the GTO emblem in its normal left side-opening location. The parking lights were mounted low beneath the outer bumper on each side.

While the front end of the '71 GTO presented a completely new impression, the remainder of the design was relatively unchanged. In fact, if you were to approach a '71 model from the rear, you would have had a hard time discerning it from a '70 model.

Even though PMD tried to downgrade the performance image that the GTO had possessed for so long, the buying public must still have made that association, and it completely turned away from the GTO. Including the final Judge, only 10,532 GTOs were constructed, which was just over a quarter of the number built in 1970. It was really hard to figure.

As had been the case in earlier years, the GTO hardtop vastly outsold the convertible, 9,497 to 661. Considering the few 455 engines that were sold, the company could just as soon have forgotten building them. The vast number of buyers bought models powered by the standard 400-ci engine. The rarity of those '71 big-block GTOs makes them very interesting collectibles in the 1990s.

1972 GTO

It was a model that was quickly getting out of step with the attitudes in America for the 1972 model year. It was the time of spiraling insurance rates, along with out-of-control emissions and safety requirements. Pontiac knew that it had to go along with the trend or fall by the wayside. The company was now calling the GTO a "road car."

The first indication that PMD was serious in this regard occurred with the cancellation of the Judge for this model year. Even if the model could be downgraded in performance, it still was talking

The standard powerplant for the '72 GTO was this 400-ci powerplant. It carried a four-barrel carburetor and dual exhausts, but the horsepower was a menial 250 net horsepower. A 455 HO was also available, this big-block being rated at 300 net horsepower.

strong with its flashy stripes. The company didn't cancel the GTO, but it gave it the ultimate slap in the face by lowering it to just an option of the LeMans line.

Such an act pointed to the possibility of the model being dropped in the near future. It was carried as the Code 334 Option Package and could be acquired with both the LeMans hardtop or Sport Convertible. The way things were going, it was enough to make a GTO buff scream!

Yet for only $344, the GTO option was still a bargain with the standard 400 engine, the heavy-duty floor-mounted three-speed, G70x14 black-wall tires, the patented Endura front end, twin hood scoops (still functional), heavy-duty shocks,

front and rear stabilizer bars, and the GTO decal identifications on the rear quarters and right rear deck locations.

It was also possible to get the GTO front end on a LeMans, along with being able to add a convertible to that LeMans, a model that you couldn't get in the GTO. The GTO powerplants could also be ordered as options to the LeMans, making it sometimes difficult to tell whether it was a LeMans or a Goat, not that most really cared.

The GTO, even though it was facing so many negatives, was still a dynamite-appearing machine, changing little from the new look that was introduced in the previous year. This styling similarity didn't happen because of corporate

With the classy front end of the '72 GTO, it was hard to differentiate the grille and front bumper. Note the deeply recessed grille openings (which are blacked out) and the low-mounted parking lights. To downgrade the prestige of the GTO, it was possible to acquire this classic front end as an option on the LeMans model.

planning, but as the result of a strike which delayed the new model.

In fact, it would be tough to tell the '71 and '72 apart, as the same Endura front end and identical mesh-filled grille openings were still in place. Differences included the so-called slotted "air extractors," which were located in the front quarters just aft of the wheelwell. The extractors would appear only during this model year. The company said the purpose of the extractors was "to keep the engine compartment cooler and reduce air pressure buildup."

Where earlier GTOs had utilized a pylon-mounted rear spoiler, available for the '72 Goat was an interesting spoiler that was integrated with the rear

deck, giving the GTO a look seen earlier in the Camaro. Stepping back to the first GTO, the exhaust used a splitter, which exited just aft of the rear wheels.

Although performance was a nasty word, there were amazingly potent ponies still being produced for the GTO. All was not lost quite yet! The 400-ci engine was still the standard engine, and it still sported a four-barrel carb and dual exhausts. Horsepower was listed as 250 net horses, which, when compared to the gross ratings of earlier years would fall into the 270-to-280 horse ratings. The 455 HO engine (the LS-5) was still on the option sheet, giving hope to the falling number of those who still wanted to scorch the tires at a stoplight.

Even though the GTO's days were numbered, this was its final year as a separate model, the Goat's interior was still as neat as you could imagine. The walnut detailing was still in place on the dash and console. It was also possible to acquire the racing-style steering wheel. It was still possible to get the macho hood-mounted tach with the '72 GTO. Its mounting position was on the left side of the hood just forward of the hood cooling slots.

Also sporting a four-barrel and duals, the top LS-5 big-block was reportedly worth 300 horsepower (maybe up to a 330 gross rating), which made the GTO a pretty effective muscle machine. Not, of course, when compared to the previous GTOs, but when compared to what was left on the muscle front, it was still standing pretty tall.

Appearance-wise, the '72 Goat didn't appear that much different from the previous year when seen from the front. But even though the look of the GTO was still in place, everybody knew that the ever-present performance was fading away.

A little tweaking on the HO, though, could produce a pretty impressive machine on street or strip. With its lowly 8.4:1 compression ratio, there was easy improvement to be made there. But there was some pretty interesting performance equipment still in place, including an aluminum intake manifold with the Ram Air system.

Interestingly, the third engine available was a standard 455 L78 mill instead of the expected small-block 400. It was rated at 250 net horsepower.

A little-known fact about the engines for the '72 Goat was that the company had considered using a hopped-up version of its 350-ci engine, to

From the side, the straight horizontal lines of the '72 GTO were very evident. First, there was the mid-side body crease, which was complemented by the lower-body chrome strip. The front fender air inlet was strictly a 1972 design feature. If you chose, and wanted to plunk down the extra money, you could acquire the classy honeycomb wheels. The wheels used a special Neothane material that was bonded to a steel disc, which in turn was welded to the wheel rim.

be called the 350 HO, and to be rated at about 284 horsepower. Hooked with a heavy-duty three-speed tranny, 3.73 rear end, and front and rear sway bars, this could have been a small-block mauler of the first order.

The plan called for the 400-ci engine to be the first optional engine, but as is known, that wouldn't be the situation. The project was dropped, and the 400 engine became the standard powerplant.

As far as external identification for the '72, the GTO decals would be omitted from the traditional front quarter position, but the GTO and engine displacement (directly underneath) would be in position on the rear quarters and right rear deck location.

Pontiac had hoped that the '72 GTO would be able to sell in the 20,000 area but hadn't figured on the changing situation with fuel and emissions considerations. In reality, the total number was just over a quarter of that anticipated figure, resting at only 5,807. Only 134 of that minimal figure were coupes, with only 10 buyers selecting the 455 HO option. Guess you'd have to say that those model/engine combinations are pretty rare in the 1990s.

The standard 400-powered hardtop coupe was the overwhelming favorite with almost 4,800 sold. A total of only 635 selected the 455 HO for the hardtop versions, with only 10 for the coupe version.

CHAPTER 3

THE FINAL GTOs, 1973–1974

For many, it was a travesty to call these final two versions GTOs. The models certainly didn't deserve the performance name that had become a legend in the 1960s.

But times were a'changing with performance becoming a bad word. The oil embargo's effects had hit the United States, with economy for getting from point A to point B being the prime consideration. Any mention of fuel-gulping big-blocks was strictly politically incorrect.

It is for those reasons that the final two GTOs had some interesting implications and were a far cry from their earlier performance brethren.

1973 GTO

Granted, the GTO name was still in place on the tenth and next-to-last GTO, but in 1973, the

The GTO letters were in place for sure, but was this really a GTO? The GTO was no longer a separate model for 1973, only an option for the LeMans model. The '73 GTO was called the "Year of the Bumper," and one look at that massive front appendage makes the name easy to understand. The Endura bumper was not able to match the new bumper standards, hence this battering-ram bumper, which looked like it had been added as an afterthought.

Out back, the differences with the previous GTOs continued. To some, the almost-flat rear deck looked pretty sharp. But that huge rear bumper sure didn't win any design contests. Note that the GTO was still in its usual location on the right rear corner of the rear deck.

famous nomenclature rated only a decal instead of chrome. Many GTO fans would indicate that's all that was deserved. One thing that it didn't deserve was to be called a model on its own, and it wasn't, again reverting back to an option of the LeMans.

Interestingly, even though the GTO was again an option, the LeMans name was nowhere to be seen on the model, with GTO decals resting on the right rear deck, lower front quarters (which also carried the engine displacement figure), and a chrome emblem in the right-side grille cutout. The GTO identification, however, was nowhere to be found in the interior. The only flair on the body included an optional stripe that cascaded down the upper fender line, coming in either red, black,

or white. The model also carried a low-mounted, front air dam, which was hardly visible.

Except from the subtle GTO changes, one would swear as he approached this GTO from the rear that it was just a LeMans. The significant differences weren't noticeable until the characteristic GTO twin grille came into view. The twin openings were characterized by very shallow recesses as opposed to the deep insets of earlier years.

You either loved or hated this one-year design, and most observers were of the latter persuasion. It did, though, have something of a sleek, muscular look about it with the smooth fastback styling and the triangular sheet metal shaping on the door panels.

Even though there were many who didn't care for the external sheet metal shaping, the interior was one sharp layout. The bench seat came stock, with bucket seats being optional.

The biggest change was the return to the 1960s-style steel bumper, which was certainly safer but it sure didn't help much from the appearance point-of-view. It destroyed the whole front end of the model and was massive enough to serve as a battering ram. It was so large and cumbersome that the bumper didn't seem to be part of the rest of the car, actually appearing to be more of an add-on item.

The bumper could be equipped with a rub-strip on its leading edge. Although the Endura bumper of the previous GTO models had remarkable recovery characteristics, it wasn't up to the 5-mile-per-hour impact criteria which this bumper needed to satisfy.

But that bumper also had one other function, to contain a pair of low-mounted cold-air scoops.

Both the Coupe and Sport Coupe (which carried louvers in the roof panel) models were available this model year with the 400-ci engine and a downgraded 455 engine. There were choices of both automatic and manual transmission options with each. The Sport Coupes were by far the most popular, with 4,312 being sold, compared to only 494 Coupe models.

The option list this year was impressive and included the following: the 400-ci four-barrel powerplant, blackout grille, dual air scoops, wide oval tires, dual exhausts, floor-mounted three-speed manual transmission, rear sway bar, 5x7-inch wheel rims, and the GTO-specific body striping and model ID trim. But the option item that really raised eyebrows were the baby moon wheel

The standard powerplant for the '73 GTO was this downgraded 400-ci powerplant, which from an appearance point-of-view was about as plain as you could get. The chrome-appearance parts that had graced earlier GTO mills were replaced by dull paint tones. And you could forget about any flashy decals on the air cleaner.

covers that looked like they had come from the local rod shop.

If the Moons didn't quite strike your fancy, also on the option list were the Rally II and flashy honeycomb wheels.

The Code T L78 400-ci powerplant was the standard mill for the penultimate next GTO, providing 230 net horsepower while operating at only an 8:1 compression ratio. There was also a 455-ci powerplant available, but again it was certainly not of the previous versions' performance levels, and certainly not the same levels as the previous Ram Air versions or the new 455 Super Duty that was being introduced with the 1973 Firebird.

In fact, some early GTO promotional material hinted that the awesome Super Duty mill might also be available for the fading GTO. The pure-race powerplant was a 310-horse stormer, which would have taken the GTO back to the good old days. But as is well known, that unfortunately would not come to pass, although there were reportedly some 120 units so equipped.

The tinkerers realized that with only a few changes, the mill could be upgraded to well over 400 horses. The performance advocates could hardly wait. Raising the stock compression ratio of 8.4:1 to over 10:1 was where much of the performance increase could have been acquired. There were also reports at the time that an aluminum block might be available, but that, too, went into the dumper.

The next-to-last GTO also sported unique tailpipe extensions that bend downward to pass by the rear bumper. Also impressive were the fake recessed hood induction scoops that appeared to be functional, but unfortunately were not!

But even though the power was downgraded from previous versions, the '73 GTO was still considered somewhat of a stormer for the time period since the performance bottom had completely dropped out with much of the competition.

And then again, with its street rod-type striping and hood scoops, the option still had a bit of a performance look about it. It had a real mean look about it even when it was just sitting there.

The optional honeycomb wheel was again available for the 1973 model year. Also note the chrome detailing around the rear wheelwell in this particular photo. The Pontiac logo was carried on the center hub of the wheel.

The buying public apparently didn't like what it saw with this model, buying only 4,806 of the next-to-last Goat. The Sport Coupe version enjoyed almost a 10:1 sales advantage over the standard coupe version, of which only 494 were sold. And although the 455 mill was an optional offering, only 25 were so equipped with the Coupe, and 519 with the Sport Coupe version. Cars with automatics again proved to be the most popular.

One can but wonder what kind of interest the '73 GTO would have attracted had the Super Duty 455 been available to be installed. It was certainly a hit with the Firebird and Trans-Am models for several years and probably would have attracted the decreasing number of performance-oriented buyers to the GTO. We can but wonder!

In the years to come, as the real performance-model GTOs dry up, this and the 1974 GTO are probably going to become more collectable.

1974 GTO: The Last One

With both fuel economy and safety shaping the engineers' thinking in the early 1970s, the GTO would take on a different complexion in its final version.

For fuel economy, downsizing was the immediate response, and the '74 GTO bore the brunt of

There was only a single powerplant available for the '74 GTO: this four-barreled 350-ci engine. A three-speed manual transmission was standard, but options included a four-speed and Turbo Hydra-Matic three-speed. A Hurst floor shifter could be acquired with the latter transmission.

the new standards, even though it still weighed in at 3,437 pounds.

Frankly, the GTO was nothing more than a deluxe version of the Ventura, which also shared Chevy Nova sheet metal. The Ventura had gone the way of many Pontiac models, starting out in the 1960s as a full-size model as an option of the Catalina line. In the early 1970s, the model would evolve into a compact as a separate model to compete with other downsized models.

Then, in 1974, the Ventura would pick up the GTO option (for only the single year) and be available in the custom coupe and hatchback series. The company literature described the machine as "Pontiac's Tough Little Road Car."

It was probably a good description because the final GTO was certainly a lot smaller than the earlier Goats, and the handling was outstanding, with the optional Radial Tuned Suspension (RTS) providing excellent responsiveness.

As the GTO was making its final bow, the GTO option sure had both some positives and some notable negatives for the performance-minded buyer. The big negative was manifested under the hood with the downgraded Code J 350-ci powerplant (rated at a menial 200 net horsepower), the only powerplant that was available this final year. It was certainly a testament as to where performance was going in the gas-shortage era, with the GTO taking one of the biggest hits.

A comparison between the final two GTOs is vividly illustrated by this photo. The sleeker '73 model is shown on the left, next to the boxier '74 version. Note that the bumper on the final GTO seems to integrate better with the grille, while the bumper on the '73 looks a lot like an afterthought.

At a time when economy was such a high priority, this low-power 350 didn't get the job done, providing only about 10 miles per gallon.

Positives of the GTO package, though, included front and rear stabilizer bars, radial-tuned stabilizer bars, radial-tuned suspension, Pliacell shocks, power steering, front and rear drum brakes, E78x14 tires, heavy-duty three-speed manual gearbox, dual exhausts with splitter extensions, 3.08:1 rear-end ratio, Rally II rims less trim rings, special grille driving lights, shaker air scoop, and computer-selected high-rate rear springs. Too bad there weren't adequate ponies to go along with those nifty features.

You've gotta admit that it was quite a pile of optional equipment for $195. But for the true GTO lover, the final Goat was an insult to the great name. How could the company do such a thing?

Since the model was really nothing special this year, why did the company even bother adorning the body with the GTO decals on the front quarters and rear deck? They were the largest GTO adornments in the history of the Goat, and several were of three-color designs. For the first time, the front-end GTO decal was carried on the right side of the hood. The long-standing GTO chrome emblem, though, was deleted from the grille this year.

There were also the expected decals on the front quarter and rear deck locations, but the engine displacement figures of the previous year were deleted.

The interior of the '74 GTO was one of the sharpest ever, even if you didn't like the look of the sheet metal. Options included bucket seats, a sport steering wheel and Rally Gauge Cluster.

Note that the gauge cluster is located on the forward end of the center console. The four gauges were angled in such a manner that they could be easily read by the driver.

Even with the back end that was often mistaken for a Chevy Nova, there was no doubt upon walking around to the front of the machine that this was a Goat, as there was the familiar Pontiac-style grille. The metal front end featured the expected double-opening style, and contained in the bumper were twin openings which fed cool air directly into the radiator.

Even with the downturn in the performance image, the last Goat still carried a functional shaker hood, a unit very similar to that carried by the Firebird and Trans Am models.

Fortunately, there was more than one tranny available besides the three-speed with a four-speed or a Turbo Hydra-Matic three-speed with a Hurst floor shifter.

You'd have to describe Goat number 11 as a Chevy with a Pontiac engine. With that in mind, the final GTO would become the only leaf-spring-suspension model, all others using coil-spring systems.

It's hard to figure, but this much-maligned GTO interrupted a series of down years by greatly outselling the previous years' models. The coupe was by far the most popular with 5,335 sold, as compared to only 1,723 for the hatchback.

And speaking of that hatchback model, there was an interesting option available which was about as far away from a performance image as you could get. It was possible to acquire a camper option: a tent-like structure could be erected out of the upraised rear-end door. The GTO as a family camping vehicle was the final insult to its proud performance history!

So it was finally over, even though many felt that these final two years didn't really deserve to be called GTOs. They were probably right.

When the final versions rolled off the production line, it marked the completion of one of the most successful runs of a special-edition performance model. The total number produced was an impressive 514,793, enabling availability of these cars well into the next century.

Of course, many GTO fans hoped that somehow the GTO would be reborn and again rival its former glory, but that would never come to pass. The

Note that the GTO emblem on the rear deck was moved from its normal right-side location. It was undoubtedly the brightest GTO emblem ever, strange since this would be the final time the famous name would be used.

The final GTO didn't really look much like a Goat, and that's because it was an option of the Ventura model. To many, it looked like a lotta Nova, understandable since it was using the same sheet metal. One owner of a final GTO actually had a license plate with the wording "NO NOVA." The functional shaker hood is also visible in this photo. The remnants of the old GTO grille were still in place for the '74 Goat. The twin grille was still there with a pair of slots being located in the substantial chrome bumper. As was the case with the '73 GTO, the Endura bumper had not returned.

name did reappear in several foreign models, but none deserved the use of the famous nomenclature.

Reportedly, PMD did consider a possible resurgence of the model with a supposed GTO-X project. The model was a downsized machine powered by a 4.9-liter turbo powerplant. Didn't happen, though.

Many GTO faithful are glad that the name was not resurrected as a sales gimmick on later models, as was done with some other performance General Motors products.

So if you really want a GTO in the 1990s, you're going to have to pay the big bucks to purchase one of the performance originals. In the years to come, the costs of these cars will continue to increase.

But if the early big-block Goats are beyond your pocketbook, you might still consider one of the final versions, which can be acquired for much more reasonable prices. Sure, they are not the machines of their brawling older brothers, but they still carry the old GTO mystique.

CHAPTER 4

THE MAGNIFICENT JUDGES, 1969-1971

Sure, everybody loved the GTO, but the characteristic that got to most of its fans was the big-time performance.

From the appearance point-of-view, though, the model was somewhat lacking in the pizzazz department compared to the competition of the era. The Goat, quite frankly, was a pretty conservative design with no neatly curved sheet metal, no fancy decals, and no body length stripes. GTO's look was more of luxury and style.

But all that went away with the advent of the Judge. Right off the bat, the name had an anti-adult sound about it. It started with its name, which came from the "Here Comes De Judge"

From the front, the first Judge (the '69 version) didn't appear to be any different from a standard GTO, but that conclusion would be deceiving. Walk around the side of the machine and the detailing differences would quickly become evident. This first Judge would be the first of three versions. The detailing for the first Judge would be considerably different from the final two versions. The classy multi-colored stripe stretched from the front of the fender and followed the line of the windows, terminating on the high rear quarter. It really spruced up the conservative GTO exterior.

GTO

75

That 60-inch-wide spoiler was one of the highlights of the first Judge. For this year only, the Judge emblem was carried on the right side of the spoiler. The spoiler featured down-turning ends that touched the rear deck. The appendage was attached to the sheet metal with a pair of pylon supports.

Judge identifiers included the attractive Judge emblem, which was carried on the front fenders and on the rear-deck spoiler. It was still a GTO, though, as that identification was in its expected left-grille-opening location.

statement that was super popular at the time. For a time, there was also a consideration to call the model "ET," for "Elapsed Time," a drag racing connotation, but we think the company made the right name choice with Judge.

OK, so the Judge was still a GTO, a highly detailed option thereof, but you certainly had to look twice to be sure of its GTO heritage. The three-year experiment really got your attention because the name of the game here was appearance. The purpose was to knock you out with the colors and graphics, and it really got the job done big-time.

All rise for The Judge.

The Judge. From Pontiac.

A new name. With a special brand of justice to discourage the so-called performance-minded competition.

Like a standard, 366-horse, 400-cubic-inch V-8 with Ram Air and a 4-barrel. Or a 370-horse, 400-cube Ram Air IV V-8, if you so order. Either way, those hood scoops function.

Like a fully synchronized, floor-mounted, 3-speed cogbox. A close-ratio 4-speed with Hurst shifter (yea!) and a 3-speed Turbo Hydra-matic (bool) are also in the hopper, if you'd care to order same.

Like a 60" air foil, blackened grille, exposed headlamps, fiber-glass belted tires (big and black), steel mag-type wheels, blue-red-yellow striping and Judge I.D. inside and out.

Like an Endura schnoz that regards chips, dings and scrapes as acts of treason.

Like Morrokide-covered buckets. And a no-nonsense instrument panel that fills you in. In detail.

Order a hood-mounted tach and power front disc brakes.

Our case rests. It's justice, man.

THE JUDGE A SPECIAL GTO BY PONTIAC

GM MARK OF EXCELLENCE
Pontiac Motor Division

The standard powerplant for the '69 Judge was the so-called Ram Air III mill, a 400-ci V-8 that provided a ground-pounding 366 horsepower. The engine carried the four-barrel Quadrajet carburetor and perked at a compression ratio of 10.75:1.

The point must be emphasized, though, that the Judge was strictly an appearance package with no special performance additions, even though it sure looked like it deserved them.

Actually, when the Judge was first introduced in 1969, it was meant to have just a one-year run to kick up GTO sales, which were starting to level off at the time. The Judge, though, would last through the 1971 model year, even though the

The performance and appearance of the first Judge were certainly applauded in this period advertisement. It mentioned both the Ram Air III and IV powerplants along with the striping and Judge emblems.

slicked-up GTO didn't do that well initially, with only 6,833 copies sold in 1969. The total wound down to 3,797 in 1970. Only 108 of the '69 Judges and 168 of the '70 models were convertibles, making them very, very desirable collectibles, as is any 1971 model, since there were only 374 produced.

As the GTO had started to pick up weight and accessories during the late 1960s, Pontiac began to consider building a modified GTO to attract the young and performance-minded buyer. The GTO had moved away from its initial performance image of the mid-1960s. There were those who felt that the muscle-car movement could last for many more years, causing the Judge production die to be cast.

The interior of the '69 Judge carried on the Pontiac tradition of macho-appearing interiors. As a part of the Judge option, the Rally Gauge Package was a nifty throw-in. This four-speed interior shows the Judge emblem, which is located on the glovebox door.

From the dead-on front view, it was hard to discern the '70 Judge from its GTO brethren. But move around to the side and the differences became obvious. The '70 Judge rates as the most popular of the three versions.

Initial Judge design deliberations considered utilizing the smaller Tempest body for the model, thus moving it completely away from the GTO family. The plan involved completely stripping down the smaller body, installing a 350 HO powerplant, and then putting it up against the hot-selling Chrysler Road Runner, a competitor which was a no-nonsense, stripped-down performance machine.

The concept, though, would be dropped in favor of simply adding a $332 option to the GTO. Also, it was decided that the 400-ci Ram Air III 366-horse powerplant would become the Judge's standard engine, with the impressive 400-ci/370-horse Ram Air IV engine being an option.

The Judge was interesting in another aspect in that the dazzling graphics and detailing were accomplished by the factory and not by an aftermarket vendor, as had been the case with other performance models of the period.

So let's check out the hows and whys of the three Judges.

The rear of the '70 Judge featured a rounded look with the bumper rolling around onto the rear quarter, bringing the taillight along with it. The Judge decal is in place in its expected location on the lower right corner of the rear deck. The smooth, clean lines of the '70 Judge rear end received raves from both customers and the car magazines alike. The rear eyebrow stripe reached to the rear bumper.

1969 Judge

The first Judge was officially released on December 19, 1968, right in the middle of the model year, and the model definitely stood out from its GTO brothers. The Judge name was announced far forward on each front fender, on the right side of the 60-inch wide rear spoiler (on convertibles only), and finally on the glovebox door. The Judge decal was a real attention-getter with red fading into black on the letters and everything completely outlined in white. Some of the first production Judges didn't have that dash emblem, instead still carrying the GTO emblem.

Some early '69 Judges also sported the stan-dard GTO chrome molding that ran the length of the lower body. These standard GTO items were used until they were depleted.

Interestingly, the GTO name was still carried forward and aft on the body. The initial Judge also featured a distinctive stripe that had the look of being fashioned in a custom rod shop of the period.

The rear deck spoiler was one of the design highlights of the model, being both functional and sporty. Interestingly, there were actually two spoiler versions for the '69 Judge, depending on whether the model was a hardtop or convertible.

In order to really attract attention, the first 2,000 '69 Judges were painted Carousel Red, but later it was possible to acquire the model in any GTO color. That same red color wouldn't even be offered the following year.

The aspect that really set off the first Judge from the two that would follow, and for that matter the whole muscle car industry at the time, was that beautiful, curving, three-color strip that swept from the top of the front fender, along the top of the door, and finally rose up to its termination on the front of the rear quarter.

Believe it, no Pontiac had ever seen something that looked like this. This was a look that really turned heads, and when combined with the Rally wheels and red-line tires, the initial Judge looked like a dolled-up Indy Pace Car model. By the way, when you think about it, it's hard to imagine that one of these Judges wasn't selected for the Brickyard honor. They, along with any of the earlier GTOs, certainly were worthy.

The bumper treatment for the first, and for that matter all of the trio of Judges, was interesting in that the front Endura flexible bumper was color-keyed with the body tone while the rear was the tried-and-true chrome.

"Ram Air" lettering on the hood announced the standard Ram Air III 400 powerplant, while "Ram Air IV" announced that awesome 400-ci/370-horse engine was in place. Recall that the Ram Air IV was a serious performance powerplant with an aluminum intake, larger exhaust ports, forged pistons, and more-efficient exhaust manifolds.

The engines were identical to those available with the standard GTOs. It is also rumored that there were a few 428-ci-powered Judges carrying Ram Air IV heads.

To maximize the performance of the model, it was possible to acquire the Saf-T-Track four-speed tranny and potent 3.90 gears in the differential.

The first Judge hit the public by storm, showing a blackout grille, integrated rear-deck spoiler, hideaway headlights, low-restriction mufflers, and Rally II wheels minus trim rings. The package came for a very reasonable $322. But you could also continue to spruce it up with a Rally Gauge package, the popular hood-mounted tach, and a num-

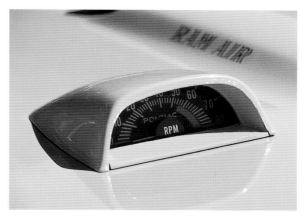

The hood tach was a part of the '70 Judge and fit in well with its overall performance image. The dial showed an 8,000-rpm range with red line occurring at 5,500. The twin hood scoops for Judge number two were similar to those on the '69 model and blended beautifully with the overall lines of the machine. The Ram Air lettering was still carried on the outside of the scoop tunnels.

ber of different rear-end axle ratios.

The very recognizable Judge decals were carried on the forward front quarters and the right side of the spoiler. Even though the first Judge set some significant appearance trends for the normally conservative GTO, the first Judge would pale in comparison to the final two versions.

To go with the looks of the '69 Judge, there was also heavy-duty suspension on the machine, which could handle the potent powerplants offered. These initial Judges stickered at $3,161 for the coupe and $4,212 for the convertible. Amazing, but true!

The hardtop was by far the most popular version with 6,725 sold and only 108 rag tops sold.

The nomenclature for the first Judge was documented under RPO 554 and UPC WT1. Recall again that the first Judge, as was the case with the final two years for the Judge, was only an option to be checked off on the GTO order form, even though it sure seemed to have acquired an identity of its own.

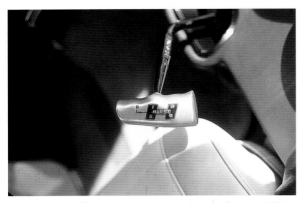

Hurst was still playing a part in the Judge in 1971 with its characteristic T-handle shifter. The corners of the 'H' carried the locations of the four-speed gears. Also, the Hurst name was emblazoned on the column.

Appearance-wise, the final Judge didn't look that much different from the '70 model. The Endura grille and flashy side graphics were still in place. This beautiful '71 example of the breed is painted in Orbit Orange, a color that wasn't available in 1971.

1970 Judge

The following year, which was really what many consider to be the final year of the muscle-car era, the Judge took on a more distinctive look with eye-catching twin eyebrow stripes front and rear. PMD engineers still had the goal of separating the Judge from its GTO brother, and with the new detailing on the '70 model, they definitely succeeded.

PMD described the Judge as "A very special GTO. Just about the wildest looking package ever to hit the street." It was certainly a statement that you couldn't argue with!

Again, the Ram Air III powerplant was the standard engine, and the optional Ram Air IV was the performance powerplant to really smoke up the bleach box at the local drag strip.

There was also a slight redesign of the rear deck spoiler for the Judge's second season with the same spoiler fitting both the hardtop and con-

vertible models. In an interesting color deviation, some of the spoilers on white '70 Judges were painted matte black while others remained white. A black gloss surface was also carried on the hood scoop ornaments for Judge number two.

The body design for the 1970 model year really fit the look of the Judge that year. It was most evident in the grille design, where the chrome grille outlines were deleted with the open-

ings being completely blacked out. Dynamite!

Additional sleekness was added to this model with a new front spoiler, again painted body color or black, whichever the customer chose.

1971 Judge

With the overall downgrade in performance, and the departure of the Judge's strongest supporters in the Pontiac corporate offices, it's not surprising that the Judge's star started to sink for what would be its last year.

Still, the company gave the final Judge its best shot. "Unless you're ready to change your image, forget our special GTO—The Judge. It's our most brazen GTO," exclaimed the company literature.

The Judge entered its final year basically unchanged appearance-wise from 1970. The same popular teardrop striping was retained, but

The biggest difference between the '70 Judge and the initial version came in the side stripe design. Where the previous model had a single stripe stretching two-thirds of the length of the body, the second Judge had two "eyebrow" stripes. It was certainly something different, detailing that had never been used before. From the side view, the '70 Judge had the look of a custom street machine. With its Rally II wheels, unique stripes, and rear-deck spoiler, this machine spoke boldly of style and performance.

the vehicle was now carrying the LS-5 455 HO 335-horse (310 net horses) powerplant, a fact that was announced on each edge of the rear spoiler.

Certain Ram Air IV components were included in that powerplant, including the aluminum intake manifold with a cast-iron crossover and tapered exhaust manifolds. The LS-5 cylinder heads, also having Ram Air similarities, sported oversized intake ports, unshrouded intake valves for better flow, and 1.76-inch-round exhaust ports. The functional Ram Air system was still in place, providing air from the twin scoops directly into the QuadraJet carburetor.

Considering that the 455 HO was operating at only 8.4:1 compression ratio, that 335-gross-horsepower figure was indeed impressive.

Standard options for the last of the Judges included the heavy-duty Muncie M20 four-speed transmission controlled by a floor-mounted Hurst shifter or the M21 Turbo Hydra-Matic. Rear-end gear ratios from 3.07:1 to 3.55:1 were available.

Suspension was still impressive on the final Judge with beefy front and rear sway bars, high-performance shocks and springs, and G70x14 belted tires.

The interior of Judge three was identical to the previous model with bucket seats, the Hurst T-handle shifter, and the Judge identification decal carried on the glovebox door. As with previous Judges, the hood-mounted tach remained popu-

An interesting location for the identification of the engine was the end of the rear-deck spoiler. It set off the racy look of the option in a big way.

lar. Also, there was a Formula steering wheel that could be acquired as an option.

The final Judge was Pontiac's last attempt to increase the declining sales of the GTO. It didn't work and the Judge was terminated in the middle of the production year, actually in February 1971. Production was extremely minimal, making these final Judges very hard to find in the 1990s. Only 357 hardtops and 17 convertibles would roll out before termination.

Like the brethren GTO base model, the '71 Judge would use the same body style, which incorporated the radical new front-end design that was a part of the GTO body updating for the model year. The relocation of the hood scoops,

which were now larger and farther forward, gave the model a completely new look—actually more of a performance look. But that would be deceiving because the ponies were quickly leaving. And again, there was that vast similarity to the sporty Firebird/Trans-Am line, whose front end almost duplicated this model.

Only 15 Judges were produced painted in a Cameo White with the striping and rear wing done in black, making them the rarest of the 1971 model. The cars were produced under an Option RPO 604, and they are highly desirable.

In terms of collectibility, the Judge rates slightly higher than the standard GTO because of its low production volume and flashy graphics. Bringing in

Note the interesting texture of the portion of the dash that carried the gauges. The walnut detailing was carried on the center console. One of the sharpest aspects of the '71 Judge interior was the racing-style steering wheel. The Pontiac symbol was carried on the center hub. The racy, hood-mounted tach was still a popular part of the overall Judge look for 1971. Located on the driver's side of the hood, it was easily read from the driver's seat.

The final Judge front end incorporated a completely integrated look. Many GTO fans think that it could really be the best-looking front on any of the Goat herd. That center hood stripe, though, was not stock.

$20,000 and more at the start of the 1990s, Judge values will continue to increase, but as is the case with all vintage muscle cars, there's just no way to predict which one will attract the attention of the collectors and jump sky high in value.

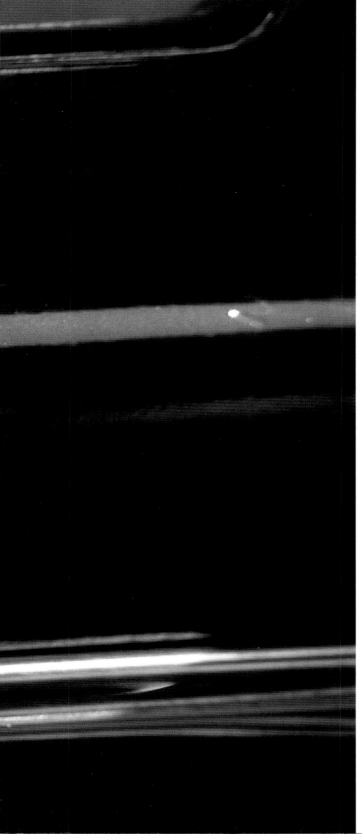

CHAPTER 5

THE ROYAL BOBCAT GTOs

During the 1960s, there was an interesting relationship between the car companies and dealers that were associated with a high-performance image. For Camaro, it was Yenko and Baldwin-Motion, and for Pontiac it came down to the Royal Pontiac dealership in Royal Oak, Michigan.

The dealership spoke street performance and had two solid activities to back it up. First of all, it was accomplished at Pontiac modifications, but it also merchandised numerous performance parts and pieces. Of significance here, though, was that it did its magic to GTOs with a number of performance packages.

During the mid-to-late 1960s, the dealership accomplished about 1,000 modifications a year, and in the 1990s, these cars are considered probably the most desirable of all the GTOs. The cars given the Royal GTO modifications carried the catchy Royal Bobcat name.

The effort was carried out by Ace Wilson, the head man at Royal Pontiac, who had PMD's approval to transform GTOs into the next realm of high performance. The ferocious machines were

This sticker was available to identify the Bobcat modification, seen here mounted on a door panel.

GTO

actually formulated and built by Milt Schornak, Royal's service manager during that golden era.

But Royal got into the performance business long before the GTO design came along. There were actually Catalinas carrying the Royal colors in national drag competition in the late 1950s. In 1960, the cars won the NHRA Stock Eliminator Class. It brought huge attention to the dealership's performance prowess.

Following that success came the Royal GP kit, which consisted of a Paxton Supercharger setup, but only a very few would be built. The so-called Tempest Tiger was a modification to a four-cylinder Tempest with a trim package and certain engine modifications. The cost was a minimal $75.

There was also experimentation by the dealership on lower-bumper induction systems similar to those used on the Olds 442 W machines, but the concept would never be adopted on GTO Bobcat modifications.

One of the most dramatic Royal packages, though, was the 421 HO Bobcat Package, a $150 option that greatly upgraded the already-potent 421 Pontiac powerplant. The conversion consisted of turning the powerplant into a full-race engine. Later, some Royal Bobcat GTOs would acquire 421s in their engine compartments resulting in 13-second quarter-mile drag machines.

But of greatest interest for this book was the GTO Bobcat kit. It should be noted from the beginning, though, that there was no company involvement in the modification of the factory-built GTOs.

Interest in such a modification was begun when two GTOs were initially modified by Royal and demonstrated screaming 13.1-second quarter-mile runs. It was the beginning of a series of Royal Bobcat GTOs, which would last until 1969 and forever hold a cherished position in the hearts of Pontiac performance fans.

When the GTO came along in 1964, it was a machine that was already a performance model before Royal got hold of it, and thoughts of how to upgrade the GTO into a killer machine came to light. Royal wanted to expose its modification skills and did so big-time by fielding a smokin' drag racing team that traveled around the country flaunting its tuning expertise.

Since there was no consistency in the way the Bobcats were marked, this emblem was seen in various locations on the cars through the Bobcat years.

It didn't take long for the word to get out that if you wanted to light your GTO performance fires, the place to buy your GTO was Royal Pontiac. And many buyers, some trekking as far as a thousand or more miles, made the trip to the Wolverine State to have that famous Royal Pontiac license plate frame on their purchase.

Most of the Royal Bobcat GTO modifications didn't carry significant external identification, but for those in the know, that little decal telling of the Bobcat breed was all that was needed.

For the 1964 and 1965 versions, the decal was carried on the base of the rear roof support. For 1966, the famous emblem would be located directly aft of the bumper on the front quarter. Later, it would move to its more familiar position just below the door handles. In 1969, it was possible to get your Bobcat endowed with a beautiful stripe job.

For example, the hood carried a double-width stripe dissecting the hood, along with racy striping reaching from upper mid-door to the top of the fenders, then dropping down and running along the lower body. The Bobcat decal was located at the body stripe starting point.

The Bobcat deviated from its company connection for the 1968 version when it was decided by the Royal staff not to adhere to Pontiac's 400-ci engine-displacement restriction. Therefore, it wasn't surprising when the performance-oriented dealership went 28 cubic inches over the company limit by installing a number of 428-ci tweaked powerplants. Reportedly, there was at least one other dealership that also installed a number of 428-ci powerplants in stock GTOs.

For the extra performance, the cost was minimal in 1990s terms, only costing an additional $650. Included in that cost was a Ram Air package for the big-block powerplant and the expected Bobcat upgrades for the new engine application.

And believe it, this baby was a rocket on the 1,320-foot strips. Reportedly, the car was capable of 104-mile-per-hour performance in high 13-second clockings, all with street equipment.

Royal Pontiac placed some interesting advertisements during those great years. They were headed by statements such as "GTO Don't Go??? They do if equipped by ROYAL," and the like. When you got right down to it, Royal Pontiac was more like a speed shop than a new car dealership.

The customer could actually upgrade his GTO in another way with the performance-oriented dealership. That is, he could do the upgrade himself with the performance parts and pieces available from Royal.

It was possible to order a complete Bobcat kit and install it on your GTO yourself. Included in the $70 package were the following components:
• Hydraulic-lifter restrictor kit
• Special carburetor jetting
• High-performance Champion spark plugs
• Blocked heat riser gaskets
• Super-thin head gaskets
• Performance centrifugal advance-curve kits

One of the more significant Royal Bobcat modifications was the introduction of a 428-ci powerplant, which replaced the standard powerplant on this 1967 model.

Reportedly, it only took about eight hours to install the kit on one's GTO. But if you lived close to Royal Pontiac, you could take your Goat in and get the package professionally installed along with equalizing the combustion chambers and milling the heads.

A comparison between a stock '67 GTO and one that carried the Royal Bobcat package was carried out by *Car Craft* magazine to check the effects of the upgrade, and the results were sizable. The stock Goat was impressive right from the dealership with low-14-second quarter-mile performance with an ET of just under 100 miles per hour. Plunk on the Bobcat kit and the new numbers were 105 miles per hour in 13.86 seconds.

Included in the kit were small Bobcat decals that could be installed on the window, showing any stoplight challenger exactly what he was up against. The popularity of the kits brought forth the formation of an enthusiasts club, the Royal Racing Club, which was initiated in 1965. At its peak in the late 1960s, the club reportedly had about 75,000 members. The Royal phenomena had reached such a point that the dealership held open houses on an annual basis to huge, appreciative crowds.

Along with its club, Royal also fielded a pack of GTO drag cars, one of which was driven by the so-called "Mystery Driver," who was wearing a tiger mask.

Pontiac was a huge benefactor from the Royal performance activities, with the car magazines performing a number of evaluations of Royal-prepared test cars. Much of the Bobcat promotion was promoted by Jim Wangers, who had pushed the GTO performance image from the beginning.

In one early snafu, a GTO not tuned by Royal was sent to a magazine, and it didn't display the performance of the Royal-prepared versions. As a result, it didn't get the glowing performance reports of the Royal Goats. Wangers was extremely upset with the downspike in his marvelous GTO performance public relations effort.

To that end, PMD released two GTOs to Wangers (who had them Royal-modified), and they were used for the next 15 magazine road tests. Wangers always made the point, though, that the cars had Royal preparation. Nonetheless, the GTO name was getting all that great preparation, and you have to wonder how many people even noted that the cars being tested weren't totally stock.

But in early 1969, as quick as it started, it was all over and owner Ace Wilson sold the complete operation to Leader Automotive. Many of the same mechanics who had performed the performance magic made the trek over to the new shop, which would continue the work, but at a lower level.

INDEX